MW01202237

From / To:

GPS Coordinates: Miles traveled:

Campground:

Address:

Site:

Check in: Check out: Cost:

- ☐ Water
- ☐ Sewer
- ☐ Electricity
- ☐ Wifi
- ☐ Fire Ring

- ☐ Easy Access
- ☐ Paved
- ☐ Restrooms
- ☐ Laundry
- ☐ Store / Cafe

☆☆☆☆☆ Location
☆☆☆☆☆ Amenities
☆☆☆☆☆ Cleanliness
☆☆☆☆☆ Security
☆☆☆☆☆ Overall

Pros / Cons:

Notes:

From / To:

GPS Coordinates: _____ Miles traveled: _____

Campground:

Address:

Site:

Check in: _____ Check out: _____ Cost: _____

☐ Water   ☐ Easy Access   ☆☆☆☆☆ Location
☐ Sewer   ☐ Paved   ☆☆☆☆☆ Amenities
☐ Electricity ☐ Restrooms   ☆☆☆☆☆ Cleanliness
☐ Wifi   ☐ Laundry   ☆☆☆☆☆ Security
☐ Fire Ring   ☐ Store / Cafe   ☆☆☆☆☆ Overall

Pros / Cons:

Notes:

From / To:

GPS Coordinates: _____ Miles traveled: _____

Campground: _____

Address: _____

Site: _____

Check in: _____ Check out: _____ Cost: _____

- ☐ Water
- ☐ Sewer
- ☐ Electricity
- ☐ Wifi
- ☐ Fire Ring

- ☐ Easy Access
- ☐ Paved
- ☐ Restrooms
- ☐ Laundry
- ☐ Store / Cafe

☆☆☆☆☆ Location
☆☆☆☆☆ Amenities
☆☆☆☆☆ Cleanliness
☆☆☆☆☆ Security
☆☆☆☆☆ Overall

Pros / Cons:

Notes:

From / To:

GPS Coordinates: _____ Miles traveled: _____

Campground: _____

Address: _____

Site: _____

Check in: _____ Check out: _____ Cost: _____

- [ ] Water
- [ ] Sewer
- [ ] Electricity
- [ ] Wifi
- [ ] Fire Ring

- [ ] Easy Access
- [ ] Paved
- [ ] Restrooms
- [ ] Laundry
- [ ] Store / Cafe

☆☆☆☆☆ Location
☆☆☆☆☆ Amenities
☆☆☆☆☆ Cleanliness
☆☆☆☆☆ Security
☆☆☆☆☆ Overall

Pros / Cons:

Notes:

From / To: _____

GPS Coordinates: _____   Miles traveled: _____

Campground: _____

Address: _____

Site: _____

Check in: _____ Check out: _____ Cost: _____

☐ Water   ☐ Easy Access   ☆☆☆☆☆ Location
☐ Sewer   ☐ Paved   ☆☆☆☆☆ Amenities
☐ Electricity ☐ Restrooms   ☆☆☆☆☆ Cleanliness
☐ Wifi   ☐ Laundry   ☆☆☆☆☆ Security
☐ Fire Ring   ☐ Store / Cafe   ☆☆☆☆☆ Overall

Pros / Cons: _____

_____

Notes: _____

_____

_____

_____

_____

_____

_____

_____

_____

_____

_____

_____

_____

_____

From / To:

GPS Coordinates: _____ Miles traveled: _____

Campground: _____

Address: _____

Site: _____

Check in: _____ Check out: _____ Cost: _____

- [ ] Water
- [ ] Sewer
- [ ] Electricity
- [ ] Wifi
- [ ] Fire Ring

- [ ] Easy Access
- [ ] Paved
- [ ] Restrooms
- [ ] Laundry
- [ ] Store / Cafe

☆☆☆☆☆ Location
☆☆☆☆☆ Amenities
☆☆☆☆☆ Cleanliness
☆☆☆☆☆ Security
☆☆☆☆☆ Overall

Pros / Cons:

Notes:

From / To:

GPS Coordinates: _____ Miles traveled: _____

Campground: _____

Address: _____

Site: _____

Check in: _____ Check out: _____ Cost: _____

☐ Water   ☐ Easy Access   ☆☆☆☆☆ Location
☐ Sewer   ☐ Paved   ☆☆☆☆☆ Amenities
☐ Electricity   ☐ Restrooms   ☆☆☆☆☆ Cleanliness
☐ Wifi   ☐ Laundry   ☆☆☆☆☆ Security
☐ Fire Ring   ☐ Store / Cafe   ☆☆☆☆☆ Overall

Pros / Cons:

Notes:

From / To:

GPS Coordinates: _____ Miles traveled: _____

Campground: _____

Address: _____

Site: _____

Check in: _____ Check out: _____ Cost: _____

☐ Water   ☐ Easy Access   ☆☆☆☆☆ Location
☐ Sewer   ☐ Paved   ☆☆☆☆☆ Amenities
☐ Electricity ☐ Restrooms   ☆☆☆☆☆ Cleanliness
☐ Wifi   ☐ Laundry   ☆☆☆☆☆ Security
☐ Fire Ring   ☐ Store / Cafe   ☆☆☆☆☆ Overall

Pros / Cons: _____

Notes: _____

From / To:

GPS Coordinates: _____ Miles traveled: _____

Campground: _____

Address: _____

Site: _____

Check in: _____ Check out: _____ Cost: _____

☐ Water   ☐ Easy Access   ☆☆☆☆☆ Location
☐ Sewer   ☐ Paved   ☆☆☆☆☆ Amenities
☐ Electricity   ☐ Restrooms   ☆☆☆☆☆ Cleanliness
☐ Wifi   ☐ Laundry   ☆☆☆☆☆ Security
☐ Fire Ring   ☐ Store / Cafe   ☆☆☆☆☆ Overall

Pros / Cons:

_____

Notes:

_____
_____
_____
_____
_____
_____
_____
_____
_____
_____
_____
_____
_____
_____
_____

From / To:

GPS Coordinates: _____ Miles traveled: _____

Campground: _____

Address: _____

Site: _____

Check in: _____ Check out: _____ Cost: _____

☐ Water   ☐ Easy Access   ☆☆☆☆☆ Location
☐ Sewer   ☐ Paved   ☆☆☆☆☆ Amenities
☐ Electricity ☐ Restrooms   ☆☆☆☆☆ Cleanliness
☐ Wifi   ☐ Laundry   ☆☆☆☆☆ Security
☐ Fire Ring   ☐ Store / Cafe   ☆☆☆☆☆ Overall

Pros / Cons: _____
_____

Notes: _____
_____
_____
_____
_____
_____
_____
_____
_____
_____
_____
_____
_____
_____
_____

From / To:

GPS Coordinates: Miles traveled:

Campground:

Address:

Site:

Check in: Check out: Cost:

☐ Water   ☐ Easy Access   ☆☆☆☆☆ Location

☐ Sewer   ☐ Paved   ☆☆☆☆☆ Amenities

☐ Electricity   ☐ Restrooms   ☆☆☆☆☆ Cleanliness

☐ Wifi   ☐ Laundry   ☆☆☆☆☆ Security

☐ Fire Ring   ☐ Store / Cafe   ☆☆☆☆☆ Overall

Pros / Cons:

Notes:

From / To:

GPS Coordinates: _____ Miles traveled: _____

Campground: _____

Address: _____

Site: _____

Check in: _____ Check out: _____ Cost: _____

☐ Water ☐ Easy Access ☆☆☆☆☆ Location

☐ Sewer ☐ Paved ☆☆☆☆☆ Amenities

☐ Electricity ☐ Restrooms ☆☆☆☆☆ Cleanliness

☐ Wifi ☐ Laundry ☆☆☆☆☆ Security

☐ Fire Ring ☐ Store / Cafe ☆☆☆☆☆ Overall

Pros / Cons:

Notes:

From / To:

GPS Coordinates: Miles traveled:

Campground:

Address:

Site:

Check in: Check out: Cost:

☐ Water   ☐ Easy Access   ☆☆☆☆☆ Location

☐ Sewer   ☐ Paved   ☆☆☆☆☆ Amenities

☐ Electricity   ☐ Restrooms   ☆☆☆☆☆ Cleanliness

☐ Wifi   ☐ Laundry   ☆☆☆☆☆ Security

☐ Fire Ring   ☐ Store / Cafe   ☆☆☆☆☆ Overall

Pros / Cons:

Notes:

From / To: _____

GPS Coordinates: _____ Miles traveled: _____

Campground: _____

Address: _____

Site: _____

Check in: _____ Check out: _____ Cost: _____

☐ Water ☐ Easy Access ☆☆☆☆☆ Location

☐ Sewer ☐ Paved ☆☆☆☆☆ Amenities

☐ Electricity ☐ Restrooms ☆☆☆☆☆ Cleanliness

☐ Wifi ☐ Laundry ☆☆☆☆☆ Security

☐ Fire Ring ☐ Store / Cafe ☆☆☆☆☆ Overall

Pros / Cons: _____

Notes: _____

From / To:

GPS Coordinates: _____ Miles traveled: _____

Campground: _____

Address: _____

Site: _____

Check in: _____ Check out: _____ Cost: _____

☐ Water   ☐ Easy Access   ☆☆☆☆☆ Location
☐ Sewer   ☐ Paved   ☆☆☆☆☆ Amenities
☐ Electricity   ☐ Restrooms   ☆☆☆☆☆ Cleanliness
☐ Wifi   ☐ Laundry   ☆☆☆☆☆ Security
☐ Fire Ring   ☐ Store / Cafe   ☆☆☆☆☆ Overall

Pros / Cons:

_____

_____

Notes:

_____
_____
_____
_____
_____
_____
_____
_____
_____
_____
_____
_____
_____
_____
_____
_____

From / To:

GPS Coordinates: _____ Miles traveled: _____

Campground: _____

Address: _____

Site: _____

Check in: _____ Check out: _____ Cost: _____

☐ Water   ☐ Easy Access   ☆☆☆☆☆ Location
☐ Sewer   ☐ Paved   ☆☆☆☆☆ Amenities
☐ Electricity   ☐ Restrooms   ☆☆☆☆☆ Cleanliness
☐ Wifi   ☐ Laundry   ☆☆☆☆☆ Security
☐ Fire Ring   ☐ Store / Cafe   ☆☆☆☆☆ Overall

Pros / Cons: _____

_____

_____

Notes: _____

_____

_____

_____

_____

_____

_____

_____

_____

_____

_____

_____

_____

_____

From / To:

GPS Coordinates: Miles traveled:

Campground:

Address:

Site:

Check in: Check out: Cost:

☐ Water   ☐ Easy Access   ☆☆☆☆☆ Location

☐ Sewer   ☐ Paved   ☆☆☆☆☆ Amenities

☐ Electricity   ☐ Restrooms   ☆☆☆☆☆ Cleanliness

☐ Wifi   ☐ Laundry   ☆☆☆☆☆ Security

☐ Fire Ring   ☐ Store / Cafe   ☆☆☆☆☆ Overall

Pros / Cons:

Notes:

From / To:

GPS Coordinates: _____ Miles traveled: _____

Campground: _____

Address: _____

Site: _____

Check in: _____ Check out: _____ Cost: _____

☐ Water   ☐ Easy Access   ☆☆☆☆☆ Location

☐ Sewer   ☐ Paved   ☆☆☆☆☆ Amenities

☐ Electricity   ☐ Restrooms   ☆☆☆☆☆ Cleanliness

☐ Wifi   ☐ Laundry   ☆☆☆☆☆ Security

☐ Fire Ring   ☐ Store / Cafe   ☆☆☆☆☆ Overall

Pros / Cons:

Notes:

From / To:

GPS Coordinates: _____ Miles traveled: _____

Campground: _____

Address: _____

Site: _____

Check in: _____ Check out: _____ Cost: _____

- ☐ Water
- ☐ Sewer
- ☐ Electricity
- ☐ Wifi
- ☐ Fire Ring

- ☐ Easy Access
- ☐ Paved
- ☐ Restrooms
- ☐ Laundry
- ☐ Store / Cafe

☆☆☆☆☆ Location
☆☆☆☆☆ Amenities
☆☆☆☆☆ Cleanliness
☆☆☆☆☆ Security
☆☆☆☆☆ Overall

Pros / Cons:

Notes:

From / To:

GPS Coordinates: Miles traveled:

Campground:

Address:

Site:

Check in: Check out: Cost:

☐ Water   ☐ Easy Access   ☆☆☆☆☆ Location

☐ Sewer   ☐ Paved   ☆☆☆☆☆ Amenities

☐ Electricity   ☐ Restrooms   ☆☆☆☆☆ Cleanliness

☐ Wifi   ☐ Laundry   ☆☆☆☆☆ Security

☐ Fire Ring   ☐ Store / Cafe   ☆☆☆☆☆ Overall

Pros / Cons:

Notes:

From / To:

GPS Coordinates: Miles traveled:

Campground:

Address:

Site:

Check in: Check out: Cost:

- [ ] Water   - [ ] Easy Access   ☆☆☆☆☆ Location
- [ ] Sewer   - [ ] Paved   ☆☆☆☆☆ Amenities
- [ ] Electricity   - [ ] Restrooms   ☆☆☆☆☆ Cleanliness
- [ ] Wifi   - [ ] Laundry   ☆☆☆☆☆ Security
- [ ] Fire Ring   - [ ] Store / Cafe   ☆☆☆☆☆ Overall

Pros / Cons:

Notes:

From / To:

GPS Coordinates: Miles traveled:

Campground:

Address:

Site:

Check in: Check out: Cost:

☐ Water   ☐ Easy Access   ☆☆☆☆☆ Location

☐ Sewer   ☐ Paved   ☆☆☆☆☆ Amenities

☐ Electricity   ☐ Restrooms   ☆☆☆☆☆ Cleanliness

☐ Wifi   ☐ Laundry   ☆☆☆☆☆ Security

☐ Fire Ring   ☐ Store / Cafe   ☆☆☆☆☆ Overall

Pros / Cons:

Notes:

From / To:

GPS Coordinates: Miles traveled:

Campground:

Address:

Site:

Check in: Check out: Cost:

☐ Water   ☐ Easy Access   ☆☆☆☆☆ Location
☐ Sewer   ☐ Paved   ☆☆☆☆☆ Amenities
☐ Electricity   ☐ Restrooms   ☆☆☆☆☆ Cleanliness
☐ Wifi   ☐ Laundry   ☆☆☆☆☆ Security
☐ Fire Ring   ☐ Store / Cafe   ☆☆☆☆☆ Overall

Pros / Cons:

Notes:

From / To:

GPS Coordinates: Miles traveled:

Campground:

Address:

Site:

Check in: Check out: Cost:

- [ ] Water   - [ ] Easy Access   ☆☆☆☆☆ Location
- [ ] Sewer   - [ ] Paved   ☆☆☆☆☆ Amenities
- [ ] Electricity   - [ ] Restrooms   ☆☆☆☆☆ Cleanliness
- [ ] Wifi   - [ ] Laundry   ☆☆☆☆☆ Security
- [ ] Fire Ring   - [ ] Store / Cafe   ☆☆☆☆☆ Overall

Pros / Cons:

Notes:

From / To:

GPS Coordinates: Miles traveled:

Campground:

Address:

Site:

Check in: Check out: Cost:

- ☐ Water
- ☐ Sewer
- ☐ Electricity
- ☐ Wifi
- ☐ Fire Ring

- ☐ Easy Access
- ☐ Paved
- ☐ Restrooms
- ☐ Laundry
- ☐ Store / Cafe

☆☆☆☆☆ Location
☆☆☆☆☆ Amenities
☆☆☆☆☆ Cleanliness
☆☆☆☆☆ Security
☆☆☆☆☆ Overall

Pros / Cons:

Notes:

From / To:

GPS Coordinates: _____ Miles traveled: _____

Campground: _____

Address: _____

Site: _____

Check in: _____ Check out: _____ Cost: _____

☐ Water   ☐ Easy Access   ☆☆☆☆☆ Location
☐ Sewer   ☐ Paved   ☆☆☆☆☆ Amenities
☐ Electricity   ☐ Restrooms   ☆☆☆☆☆ Cleanliness
☐ Wifi   ☐ Laundry   ☆☆☆☆☆ Security
☐ Fire Ring   ☐ Store / Cafe   ☆☆☆☆☆ Overall

Pros / Cons:

_____

_____

Notes:

_____
_____
_____
_____
_____
_____
_____
_____
_____
_____
_____
_____
_____
_____
_____
_____

From / To:

GPS Coordinates: _____ Miles traveled: _____

Campground: _____

Address: _____

Site: _____

Check in: _____ Check out: _____ Cost: _____

☐ Water   ☐ Easy Access   ☆☆☆☆☆ Location
☐ Sewer   ☐ Paved   ☆☆☆☆☆ Amenities
☐ Electricity ☐ Restrooms   ☆☆☆☆☆ Cleanliness
☐ Wifi   ☐ Laundry   ☆☆☆☆☆ Security
☐ Fire Ring   ☐ Store / Cafe   ☆☆☆☆☆ Overall

Pros / Cons:

_____

_____

Notes:

_____

_____

_____

_____

_____

_____

_____

_____

_____

_____

_____

_____

_____

_____

From / To:

GPS Coordinates: Miles traveled:

Campground:

Address:

Site:

Check in: Check out: Cost:

☐ Water   ☐ Easy Access   ☆☆☆☆☆ Location

☐ Sewer   ☐ Paved   ☆☆☆☆☆ Amenities

☐ Electricity   ☐ Restrooms   ☆☆☆☆☆ Cleanliness

☐ Wifi   ☐ Laundry   ☆☆☆☆☆ Security

☐ Fire Ring   ☐ Store / Cafe   ☆☆☆☆☆ Overall

Pros / Cons:

Notes:

From / To:

GPS Coordinates: Miles traveled:

Campground:

Address:

Site:

Check in: Check out: Cost:

☐ Water   ☐ Easy Access   ☆☆☆☆☆ Location
☐ Sewer   ☐ Paved   ☆☆☆☆☆ Amenities
☐ Electricity   ☐ Restrooms   ☆☆☆☆☆ Cleanliness
☐ Wifi   ☐ Laundry   ☆☆☆☆☆ Security
☐ Fire Ring   ☐ Store / Cafe   ☆☆☆☆☆ Overall

Pros / Cons:

Notes:

From / To:

GPS Coordinates: Miles traveled:

Campground:

Address:

Site:

Check in: Check out: Cost:

☐ Water   ☐ Easy Access   ☆☆☆☆☆ Location

☐ Sewer   ☐ Paved   ☆☆☆☆☆ Amenities

☐ Electricity   ☐ Restrooms   ☆☆☆☆☆ Cleanliness

☐ Wifi   ☐ Laundry   ☆☆☆☆☆ Security

☐ Fire Ring   ☐ Store / Cafe   ☆☆☆☆☆ Overall

Pros / Cons:

Notes:

From / To: _____

GPS Coordinates: _____ Miles traveled: _____

Campground: _____

Address: _____

Site: _____

Check in: _____ Check out: _____ Cost: _____

☐ Water   ☐ Easy Access   ☆☆☆☆☆ Location
☐ Sewer   ☐ Paved   ☆☆☆☆☆ Amenities
☐ Electricity ☐ Restrooms   ☆☆☆☆☆ Cleanliness
☐ Wifi   ☐ Laundry   ☆☆☆☆☆ Security
☐ Fire Ring   ☐ Store / Cafe ☆☆☆☆☆ Overall

Pros / Cons: _____

Notes: _____

From / To:

GPS Coordinates: _____ Miles traveled: _____

Campground: _____

Address: _____

Site: _____

Check in: _____ Check out: _____ Cost: _____

☐ Water   ☐ Easy Access   ☆☆☆☆☆ Location
☐ Sewer   ☐ Paved   ☆☆☆☆☆ Amenities
☐ Electricity   ☐ Restrooms   ☆☆☆☆☆ Cleanliness
☐ Wifi   ☐ Laundry   ☆☆☆☆☆ Security
☐ Fire Ring   ☐ Store / Cafe   ☆☆☆☆☆ Overall

Pros / Cons:

_____

_____

Notes:

_____

_____

_____

_____

_____

_____

_____

_____

_____

_____

_____

_____

_____

From / To:

GPS Coordinates: Miles traveled:

Campground:

Address:

Site:

Check in: Check out: Cost:

- ☐ Water
- ☐ Sewer
- ☐ Electricity
- ☐ Wifi
- ☐ Fire Ring

- ☐ Easy Access
- ☐ Paved
- ☐ Restrooms
- ☐ Laundry
- ☐ Store / Cafe

☆☆☆☆☆ Location
☆☆☆☆☆ Amenities
☆☆☆☆☆ Cleanliness
☆☆☆☆☆ Security
☆☆☆☆☆ Overall

Pros / Cons:

Notes:

From / To: _____

GPS Coordinates: _____ Miles traveled: _____

Campground: _____

Address: _____

Site: _____

Check in: _____ Check out: _____ Cost: _____

☐ Water   ☐ Easy Access   ☆☆☆☆☆ Location
☐ Sewer   ☐ Paved   ☆☆☆☆☆ Amenities
☐ Electricity   ☐ Restrooms   ☆☆☆☆☆ Cleanliness
☐ Wifi   ☐ Laundry   ☆☆☆☆☆ Security
☐ Fire Ring   ☐ Store / Cafe   ☆☆☆☆☆ Overall

Pros / Cons:
_____
_____

Notes:
_____
_____
_____
_____
_____
_____
_____
_____
_____
_____
_____
_____
_____
_____
_____

From / To: _____

GPS Coordinates: _____ Miles traveled: _____

Campground: _____

Address: _____

Site: _____

Check in: _____ Check out: _____ Cost: _____

☐ Water   ☐ Easy Access   ☆☆☆☆☆ Location

☐ Sewer   ☐ Paved   ☆☆☆☆☆ Amenities

☐ Electricity   ☐ Restrooms   ☆☆☆☆☆ Cleanliness

☐ Wifi   ☐ Laundry   ☆☆☆☆☆ Security

☐ Fire Ring   ☐ Store / Cafe   ☆☆☆☆☆ Overall

Pros / Cons: _____

_____

Notes: _____

From / To:

GPS Coordinates: Miles traveled:

Campground:

Address:

Site:

Check in: Check out: Cost:

☐ Water   ☐ Easy Access   ☆☆☆☆☆ Location

☐ Sewer   ☐ Paved   ☆☆☆☆☆ Amenities

☐ Electricity   ☐ Restrooms   ☆☆☆☆☆ Cleanliness

☐ Wifi   ☐ Laundry   ☆☆☆☆☆ Security

☐ Fire Ring   ☐ Store / Cafe   ☆☆☆☆☆ Overall

Pros / Cons:

Notes:

From / To:

GPS Coordinates: _____ Miles traveled: _____

Campground: _____

Address: _____

Site: _____

Check in: _____ Check out: _____ Cost: _____

☐ Water   ☐ Easy Access   ☆☆☆☆☆ Location

☐ Sewer   ☐ Paved   ☆☆☆☆☆ Amenities

☐ Electricity   ☐ Restrooms   ☆☆☆☆☆ Cleanliness

☐ Wifi   ☐ Laundry   ☆☆☆☆☆ Security

☐ Fire Ring   ☐ Store / Cafe   ☆☆☆☆☆ Overall

Pros / Cons: _____

_____

Notes: _____

_____

_____

_____

_____

_____

_____

_____

_____

_____

_____

_____

_____

_____

_____

_____

From / To:

GPS Coordinates: Miles traveled:

Campground:

Address:

Site:

Check in: Check out: Cost:

☐ Water   ☐ Easy Access   ☆☆☆☆☆ Location

☐ Sewer   ☐ Paved   ☆☆☆☆☆ Amenities

☐ Electricity   ☐ Restrooms   ☆☆☆☆☆ Cleanliness

☐ Wifi   ☐ Laundry   ☆☆☆☆☆ Security

☐ Fire Ring   ☐ Store / Cafe   ☆☆☆☆☆ Overall

Pros / Cons:

Notes:

From / To:

GPS Coordinates: _____ Miles traveled: _____

Campground: _____

Address: _____

Site: _____

Check in: _____ Check out: _____ Cost: _____

☐ Water   ☐ Easy Access   ☆☆☆☆☆ Location

☐ Sewer   ☐ Paved   ☆☆☆☆☆ Amenities

☐ Electricity   ☐ Restrooms   ☆☆☆☆☆ Cleanliness

☐ Wifi   ☐ Laundry   ☆☆☆☆☆ Security

☐ Fire Ring   ☐ Store / Cafe   ☆☆☆☆☆ Overall

Pros / Cons:

_____
_____

Notes:

_____
_____
_____
_____
_____
_____
_____
_____
_____
_____
_____
_____
_____
_____

From / To:

GPS Coordinates: Miles traveled:

Campground:

Address:

Site:

Check in: Check out: Cost:

☐ Water   ☐ Easy Access   ☆☆☆☆☆ Location
☐ Sewer   ☐ Paved   ☆☆☆☆☆ Amenities
☐ Electricity   ☐ Restrooms   ☆☆☆☆☆ Cleanliness
☐ Wifi   ☐ Laundry   ☆☆☆☆☆ Security
☐ Fire Ring   ☐ Store / Cafe   ☆☆☆☆☆ Overall

Pros / Cons:

Notes:

From / To:

GPS Coordinates: Miles traveled:

Campground:

Address:

Site:

Check in: Check out: Cost:

☐ Water   ☐ Easy Access   ☆☆☆☆☆ Location
☐ Sewer   ☐ Paved   ☆☆☆☆☆ Amenities
☐ Electricity   ☐ Restrooms   ☆☆☆☆☆ Cleanliness
☐ Wifi   ☐ Laundry   ☆☆☆☆☆ Security
☐ Fire Ring   ☐ Store / Cafe   ☆☆☆☆☆ Overall

Pros / Cons:

Notes:

From / To:

GPS Coordinates: .... Miles traveled: ....

Campground: ....

Address: ....

Site: ....

Check in: .... Check out: .... Cost: ....

☐ Water   ☐ Easy Access   ☆☆☆☆☆ Location
☐ Sewer   ☐ Paved   ☆☆☆☆☆ Amenities
☐ Electricity   ☐ Restrooms   ☆☆☆☆☆ Cleanliness
☐ Wifi   ☐ Laundry   ☆☆☆☆☆ Security
☐ Fire Ring   ☐ Store / Cafe   ☆☆☆☆☆ Overall

Pros / Cons:

Notes:

From / To:

GPS Coordinates: _____ Miles traveled: _____

Campground: _____

Address: _____

Site: _____

Check in: _____ Check out: _____ Cost: _____

☐ Water   ☐ Easy Access   ☆☆☆☆☆ Location
☐ Sewer   ☐ Paved   ☆☆☆☆☆ Amenities
☐ Electricity ☐ Restrooms   ☆☆☆☆☆ Cleanliness
☐ Wifi   ☐ Laundry   ☆☆☆☆☆ Security
☐ Fire Ring   ☐ Store / Cafe   ☆☆☆☆☆ Overall

Pros / Cons:

Notes:

From / To:

GPS Coordinates: Miles traveled:

Campground:

Address:

Site:

Check in: Check out: Cost:

☐ Water   ☐ Easy Access   ☆☆☆☆☆ Location

☐ Sewer   ☐ Paved   ☆☆☆☆☆ Amenities

☐ Electricity   ☐ Restrooms   ☆☆☆☆☆ Cleanliness

☐ Wifi   ☐ Laundry   ☆☆☆☆☆ Security

☐ Fire Ring   ☐ Store / Cafe   ☆☆☆☆☆ Overall

Pros / Cons:

Notes:

From / To:

GPS Coordinates: _____ Miles traveled: _____

Campground: _____

Address: _____

Site: _____

Check in: _____ Check out: _____ Cost: _____

☐ Water   ☐ Easy Access   ☆☆☆☆☆ Location
☐ Sewer   ☐ Paved   ☆☆☆☆☆ Amenities
☐ Electricity   ☐ Restrooms   ☆☆☆☆☆ Cleanliness
☐ Wifi   ☐ Laundry   ☆☆☆☆☆ Security
☐ Fire Ring   ☐ Store / Cafe   ☆☆☆☆☆ Overall

Pros / Cons:

Notes:

From / To:

GPS Coordinates: Miles traveled:

Campground:

Address:

Site:

Check in: Check out: Cost:

☐ Water	☐ Easy Access	☆☆☆☆☆ Location
☐ Sewer	☐ Paved	☆☆☆☆☆ Amenities
☐ Electricity	☐ Restrooms	☆☆☆☆☆ Cleanliness
☐ Wifi	☐ Laundry	☆☆☆☆☆ Security
☐ Fire Ring	☐ Store / Cafe	☆☆☆☆☆ Overall

Pros / Cons:

Notes:

From / To:

GPS Coordinates: _____ Miles traveled: _____

Campground: _____

Address: _____

Site: _____

Check in: _____ Check out: _____ Cost: _____

- [ ] Water
- [ ] Sewer
- [ ] Electricity
- [ ] Wifi
- [ ] Fire Ring

- [ ] Easy Access
- [ ] Paved
- [ ] Restrooms
- [ ] Laundry
- [ ] Store / Cafe

☆☆☆☆☆ Location
☆☆☆☆☆ Amenities
☆☆☆☆☆ Cleanliness
☆☆☆☆☆ Security
☆☆☆☆☆ Overall

Pros / Cons:

Notes:

From / To:

GPS Coordinates: Miles traveled:

Campground:

Address:

Site:

Check in: Check out: Cost:

☐ Water   ☐ Easy Access   ☆☆☆☆☆ Location
☐ Sewer   ☐ Paved   ☆☆☆☆☆ Amenities
☐ Electricity   ☐ Restrooms   ☆☆☆☆☆ Cleanliness
☐ Wifi   ☐ Laundry   ☆☆☆☆☆ Security
☐ Fire Ring   ☐ Store / Cafe   ☆☆☆☆☆ Overall

Pros / Cons:

Notes:

From / To:

GPS Coordinates: _____ Miles traveled: _____

Campground: _____

Address: _____

Site: _____

Check in: _____ Check out: _____ Cost: _____

☐ Water   ☐ Easy Access   ☆☆☆☆☆ Location
☐ Sewer   ☐ Paved   ☆☆☆☆☆ Amenities
☐ Electricity ☐ Restrooms   ☆☆☆☆☆ Cleanliness
☐ Wifi   ☐ Laundry   ☆☆☆☆☆ Security
☐ Fire Ring   ☐ Store / Cafe   ☆☆☆☆☆ Overall

Pros / Cons:

Notes:

From / To:

GPS Coordinates: Miles traveled:

Campground:

Address:

Site:

Check in: Check out: Cost:

☐ Water   ☐ Easy Access   ☆☆☆☆☆ Location

☐ Sewer   ☐ Paved   ☆☆☆☆☆ Amenities

☐ Electricity   ☐ Restrooms   ☆☆☆☆☆ Cleanliness

☐ Wifi   ☐ Laundry   ☆☆☆☆☆ Security

☐ Fire Ring   ☐ Store / Cafe   ☆☆☆☆☆ Overall

Pros / Cons:

Notes:

From / To:

GPS Coordinates: Miles traveled:

Campground:

Address:

Site:

Check in: Check out: Cost:

- [ ] Water   - [ ] Easy Access   ☆☆☆☆☆ Location
- [ ] Sewer   - [ ] Paved   ☆☆☆☆☆ Amenities
- [ ] Electricity   - [ ] Restrooms   ☆☆☆☆☆ Cleanliness
- [ ] Wifi   - [ ] Laundry   ☆☆☆☆☆ Security
- [ ] Fire Ring   - [ ] Store / Cafe   ☆☆☆☆☆ Overall

Pros / Cons:

Notes:

From / To:

GPS Coordinates: _____ Miles traveled: _____

Campground: _____

Address: _____

Site: _____

Check in: _____ Check out: _____ Cost: _____

☐ Water   ☐ Easy Access   ☆☆☆☆☆ Location
☐ Sewer   ☐ Paved   ☆☆☆☆☆ Amenities
☐ Electricity   ☐ Restrooms   ☆☆☆☆☆ Cleanliness
☐ Wifi   ☐ Laundry   ☆☆☆☆☆ Security
☐ Fire Ring   ☐ Store / Cafe   ☆☆☆☆☆ Overall

Pros / Cons:

_____

_____

Notes:

_____
_____
_____
_____
_____
_____
_____
_____
_____
_____
_____
_____
_____
_____
_____

From / To:

GPS Coordinates: _____ Miles traveled: _____

Campground: _____

Address: _____

Site: _____

Check in: _____ Check out: _____ Cost: _____

☐ Water   ☐ Easy Access   ☆☆☆☆☆ Location
☐ Sewer   ☐ Paved   ☆☆☆☆☆ Amenities
☐ Electricity   ☐ Restrooms   ☆☆☆☆☆ Cleanliness
☐ Wifi   ☐ Laundry   ☆☆☆☆☆ Security
☐ Fire Ring   ☐ Store / Cafe   ☆☆☆☆☆ Overall

Pros / Cons:
_____
_____
_____

Notes:
_____
_____
_____
_____
_____
_____
_____
_____
_____
_____
_____
_____
_____
_____

From / To:

GPS Coordinates: _____ Miles traveled: _____

Campground: _____

Address: _____

Site: _____

Check in: _____ Check out: _____ Cost: _____

☐ Water   ☐ Easy Access   ☆☆☆☆☆ Location
☐ Sewer   ☐ Paved   ☆☆☆☆☆ Amenities
☐ Electricity ☐ Restrooms   ☆☆☆☆☆ Cleanliness
☐ Wifi   ☐ Laundry   ☆☆☆☆☆ Security
☐ Fire Ring ☐ Store / Cafe   ☆☆☆☆☆ Overall

Pros / Cons:

Notes:

Made in the USA
Middletown, DE
05 September 2019